CODE READER™

Making Difficult Words Easy

Code Reader Books provide codes with "sound keys" to help read difficult words. For example, a word that may be difficult to read is "unicorn," so it might be followed by a code like this: unicorn *(YOO-nih-korn)*. By providing codes with phonetic sound keys, Code Reader Books make reading easier and more enjoyable.

Examples of Code Reader™ Keys

Long a sound (as in make):
a *(with a silent e)* or **ay**
Examples: able *(AY-bul)*; break *(brake)*

Short i sound (as in sit): **i** or **ih**
Examples: myth *(mith)*; mission *(MIH-shun)*

Long i sound (as in by):
i *(with a silent e)* or **y**
Examples: might *(mite)*; bicycle *(BY-sih-kul)*

Keys for the long o sound (as in hope):
o *(with a silent e)* or **oh**
Examples: molten *(MOLE-ten)*; ocean *(OH-shen)*

Codes use dashes between syllables *(SIH-luh-buls)*, and stressed syllables have capital letters.

To see more Code Reader sound keys, see page 44.

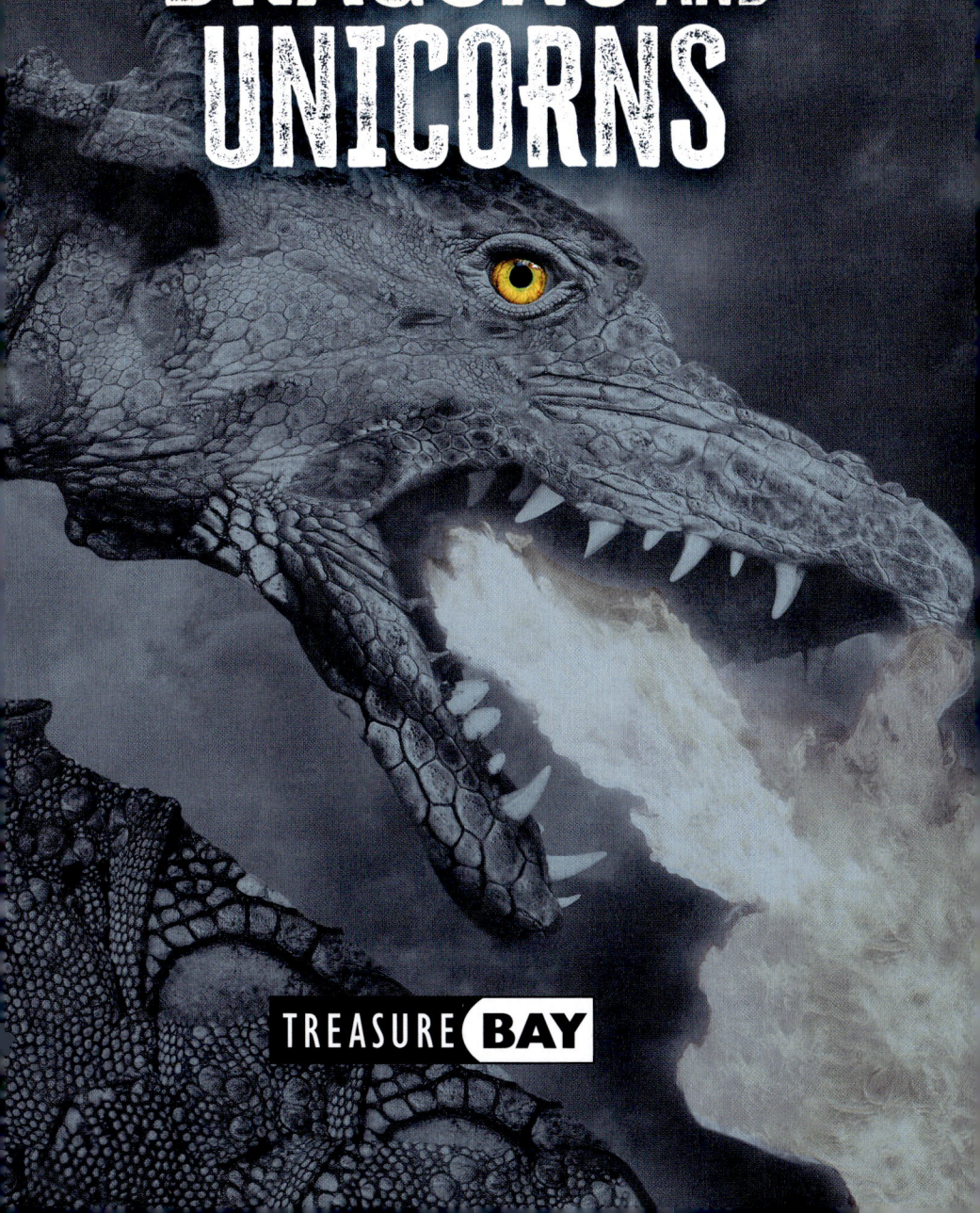

Dragons and Unicorns
A Code Reader™ Chapter Book
Blue Series

This book, along with images and text, is published
under license from The Creative Company. Originally published
as Unicorns and Dragons © 2020 Creative Education,
Creative Paperbacks and Curious About Dragons and
Curious About Unicorns © 2023 Amicus

Additions and revisions to text in this licensed edition:
Copyright © 2025 Treasure Bay, Inc.
Additional images provided by iStock

Reading Consultant: Jennifer L. VanSlander, Ph.D., Asst. Professor
of Educational Leadership, Columbus State University

Code Reader™ is a trademark of Treasure Bay, Inc.

Patent Pending.
Code Reader books are designed using an innovative system of methods
to create and include phonetic codes to enhance the readability of text.
Reserved rights include any patent rights.

Published by
Treasure Bay, Inc.
PO Box 519
Roseville, CA 95661 USA

Printed in China

Library of Congress Control Number: 2024944962

ISBN: 978-1-60115-727-0

Visit us online at:
CodeReader.org

PR-1-25

CONTENTS

CHAPTER 1

MYTHICAL ANIMALS
(MITH-ih-kul)

For thousands of years, people created myths *(miths)* and legends *(LEH-jindz)* to help them define the world around them. These stories helped them explain things that they did not yet understand. Many myths and legends include mythical *(MITH-ih-kul)* animals. The stories describe the impact these imaginary *(im-MAJ-ih-nare-ee)* creatures *(KREE-churz)* have on humans and how humans interact with them.

Mythical creatures come in all shapes, colors, and sizes. Many, such as the Greek Minotaur *(MIN-uh-tar)*, take the form of hybrids *(HY-bridz)*. A hybrid is a combination of two different animals. The Minotaur *(MIN-uh-tar)* is depicted as half-bull and half-human.

Some, like the Kraken *(KRAK-un)*, may take the form of a larger, more dangerous *(DANE-jer-us)* version of an existing animal. The Kraken, a creature similar to a giant squid *(skwid)*, was said to be huge and powerful enough to pull an entire ship down to its doom.

Still others, like the half-fish, half-human mermaid, have specific *(speh-SIF-ik)* magical powers. The mermaids' beautiful voices are thought to have the power to lure sailors to their death on the rocks where the mermaids sit and sing.

Two of the most fascinating *(FAS-ih-nay-ting)* mythical creatures are unicorns and dragons. Stories of these creatures exist in cultures *(KUL-churz)* all over the world.

Legends *(LEH-jinz)* of unicorns go back more than 2,000 years. Most describe unicorns as white horses that have a single, spiraling *(SPY-ruh-ling)* horn growing on their forehead. Anyone who touches a pure white unicorn is said to have a happy and blessed life.

The oldest records of dragons describe snake-like beasts that were evil and very frightening *(FRY-tih-ning)*. It was thought that these beasts had poisonous *(POY-zuh-nus)* blood *(blud)* and that touching their blood would cause instant death.

CHAPTER 2

WHAT IS A UNICORN?

The true origin *(OR-ih-jin)* of the unicorn myths is not known, but unicorns can be found in stories from all over the world. In almost all cases, they represent innocence *(IN-uh-sens)*, power, and magic.

Thousands of years ago, a Greek traveler wrote about exotic places. He claimed to have seen unicorns. He said they looked something like a donkey with a white body and a red head.

Throughout (throo-OWT) history, many unique (yoo-NEEK) animals have been mistaken for unicorns. The oryx (OR-ix) is a type of antelope with a horse-like neck and mane. It has long horns with rings that can look like spirals (SPY-rulz). When seen from the side, these long horns can look like one single horn. You can see how the Greek traveler may have been fooled into thinking it was one horn. Or maybe he saw an oryx that had lost one of its horns!

Rhinoceroses *(ry-NOS-ur-us-ez)* do not look at all like horses, but certain *(SER-tin)* types do have only one horn, low on their face. Some think rhinos were sometimes mistaken for unicorns as well.

Different cultures *(KUL-churz)* have different ideas *(I-DEE-uhz)* of what these creatures looked like. They may also have different names depending on the country.

QILIN / KILIN (CHINA *(CHY-nuh)*)

EUROPEAN UNICORN *(yur-ruh-PEE-en)*

INDIAN UNICORN *(IN-dee-en)*

KIRIN (JAPAN *(juh-PAN)*)

PEGACORN (ANCIENT *(AIN-chent)* ROME)

Unicorns are believed *(buh-LEEVD)* to make their homes somewhere deep in dense *(dens)* forests. They are said to live near lakes and ponds. Sometimes unicorns will stop in clearings in the forest to rest. That's where people would claim to see them. But unicorns have a keen sense of hearing, so humans cannot sneak up on them undetected *(un-dee-TEK-ted)*. A unicorn will always know.

Most of these mythical creatures have stunning purple or blue eyes. Legend says that, if you look into a unicorn's eyes, you will see the unicorn's forest home.

Horses often have only one baby at a time. Unicorns probably would, too.

Unicorns do not eat food. Instead, it is believed that they get their energy *(EN-er-jee)* from the sun. They are known to have strong hearts and can live for hundreds of years.

A group of unicorns is called a blessing.

CHAPTER 3

UNICORN SKILLS

All unicorns have one horn, but the body may be different depending on the legend. Myths in some parts of the world said unicorns had wings. European *(yur-uh-PEE-un)* unicorns usually *(YOO-zhoo-uh-lee)* look like horses or goats.

In China *(CHY-nuh)* and Japan *(juh-PAN)*, they tend to look like deer with dragon heads. Unicorns in India *(IN-dee-uh)* may have red and black horns. Myths of Chinese unicorns said they could tell the future *(FYOO-chur)* and breathe fire!

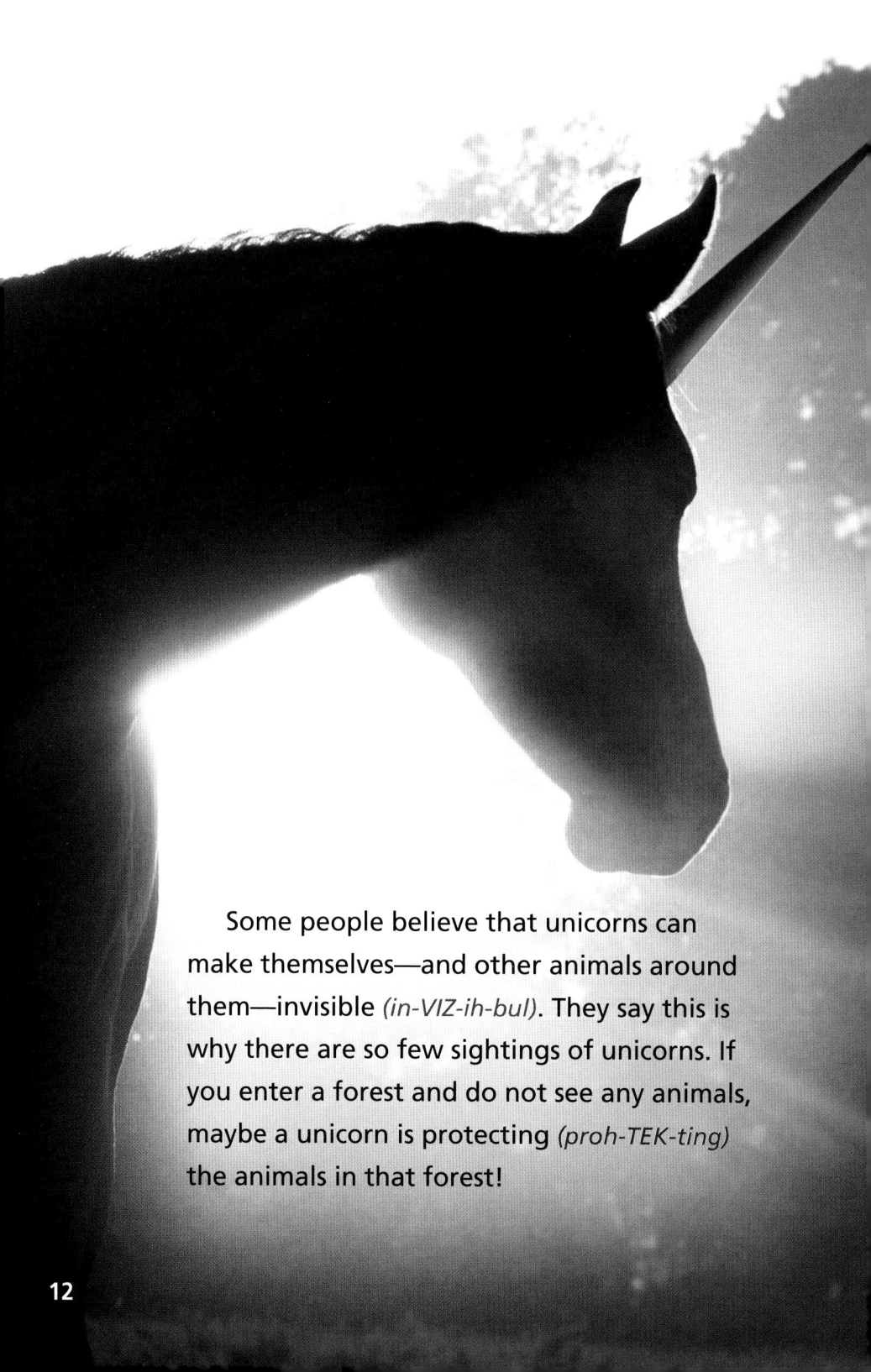

Some people believe that unicorns can make themselves—and other animals around them—invisible *(in-VIZ-ih-bul)*. They say this is why there are so few sightings of unicorns. If you enter a forest and do not see any animals, maybe a unicorn is protecting *(proh-TEK-ting)* the animals in that forest!

It is said that these creatures can run faster than the speed of light. The speed of light is 186,282 miles per second *(SEK-unt)*! Legend tells us that, even if you could catch a unicorn, it would be impossible *(im-POS-sih-bul)* to tame.

Unicorn horns are called alicorns *(AL-ih-kornz)*. In most stories, a unicorn's magic comes from its horn.

A unicorn's horn, or an alicorn *(AL-ih-korn)*, is said to take away poison *(POY-zun)*, so kings and queens drank from cups that they were told were made from unicorn horns. They thought no one could poison their drinks this way. In truth, these cups were probably made from narwhal *(NAR-wol)* tusks.

The narwhal *(NAR-wol)* is a real animal. Narwhals are small whales that have a long, forward-pointing spiral *(SPY-rul)* tusk that can be ten feet long! Narwhals are often nicknamed "unicorns of the sea."

It was believed that, when alicorns (unicorn horns) were ground into a powder, the powder could cure illnesses. Alicorn powder was used in medicine *(MED-ih-sin)* as recently *(REE-sent-lee)* as 1741. But this powder was probably ground from either a narwhal tusk or the horn of a rhinoceros or other animal.

INDIAN RHINO

SIBERIAN UNICORN (EXTINCT)

NARWHAL

CHAPTER 4

UNICORN LEGENDS

Although *(awl-THOH)* unicorns are usually viewed as gentle *(JEN-tul)*, they can also be fierce *(FEERes)* fighters. Some legends say unicorns battled elephants *(EL-eh-fents)* and lions. And the unicorns usually won these battles. The United *(yoo-NY-ted)* Kingdom's coat of arms contains a lion and a unicorn. The lion represents *(rep-ree-ZENTS)* England *(ING-glund)*. The unicorn represents Scotland.

Long ago, England and Scotland fought. Known for its strength, the lion became the symbol for England in the 12th century. But unicorns are said to be able to defeat lions. So, Scotland adopted the mythical creature as its national *(NASH-uh-nul)* animal in the 14th century.

The Turkish kartijan *(KAR-tih-jin)* was a ferocious *(fur-OH-shus)* unicorn. It was huge. The sound of its hooves was like thunder across the land. Perhaps this myth was based on the rhinoceros.

Italian *(ih-TAL-yin)* explorer Marco Polo *(POH-loh)* traveled to China in the late 1200s. He wrote about incredible *(in-KRED-ih-bul)* and exotic beasts he saw along the way. He believed he saw unicorns. He described them as big elephants with a horn. He said they lazed in the mud and kept their heads low like wild boars. Marco Polo concluded these unicorns were ugly and nothing like the shining white unicorns of folk tales. The animals he described were likely rhinoceroses, but we will never know for sure exactly what he saw.

In many stories, unicorns only let young women *(WIH-men)* come near them.

In one European *(yur-ruh-PEE-en)* fairy tale, hunters try to catch a white unicorn, but it is too swift to be caught *(cawt)*. So, hunters set a trap. They bring a young maiden into the forest. The unicorn is drawn to her. It puts its head in her lap. As she combs *(cohmz)* its mane, it falls asleep. The hunters move in to catch it and take it to the king. But the unicorn escapes and runs back to the forest.

The Last Unicorn is a popular *(POP-yoo-lur)* book written by Peter S. Beagle *(BEE-gul)*, published in 1968. In this story, a unicorn hears that a bull has captured *(KAP-churd)* all the other unicorns. She leaves her forest home to rescue *(RES-kyoo)* her fellow unicorns. Her journey *(JER-nee)* is filled with danger *(DANE-jer)*, but she makes friends along the way.

CHAPTER 5

WATATSUMI
(wah-tat-SOO-mee)

(Japanese Myth)
(ja-puh-NEEZ)

WHAT IS A DRAGON?

As beautiful and mysterious *(mis-TEER-ee-us)* as the unicorn is, the mythical dragon is equally *(EE-kwul-lee)* as fascinating *(FAS-ih-nay-ting)*. The word "dragon" comes from the Greek word drakon *(DRAK-ohn),* which describes any large serpent, or large snake. But where did the whole idea of a dragon come from in the first place?

Scholars *(SKAH-lurz)* say that belief in dragons probably evolved independently in both Europe *(YUR-rup)* and China, and perhaps in the Americas and Australia *(ah-STRAYL-yuh)* as well. European dragons are often dinosaur-like while Asian *(AY-zhun)* dragons look more like serpents, or snakes.

DRAGON
(European Myth)

FIRE SERPENT
(Aztec Myth)

HYDRA
(HY-druh)
(Greek Myth)

Some think that real animals may have inspired the first dragon legends. Long ago, people *(PEE-pul)* found the bones and fossils of dinosaurs. Having no idea what kind of animal the bones really came from, they created *(kree-AY-ted)* the idea of dragons to explain them.

The Nile crocodile *(KROK-uh-dile)* is another animal that might be mistaken for a dragon. These huge *(hyooj)* reptiles can be up to eighteen feet long. A Nile crocodile will sometimes do what is called a "high walk," where it lifts its body and tail off the ground while walking on its short legs.

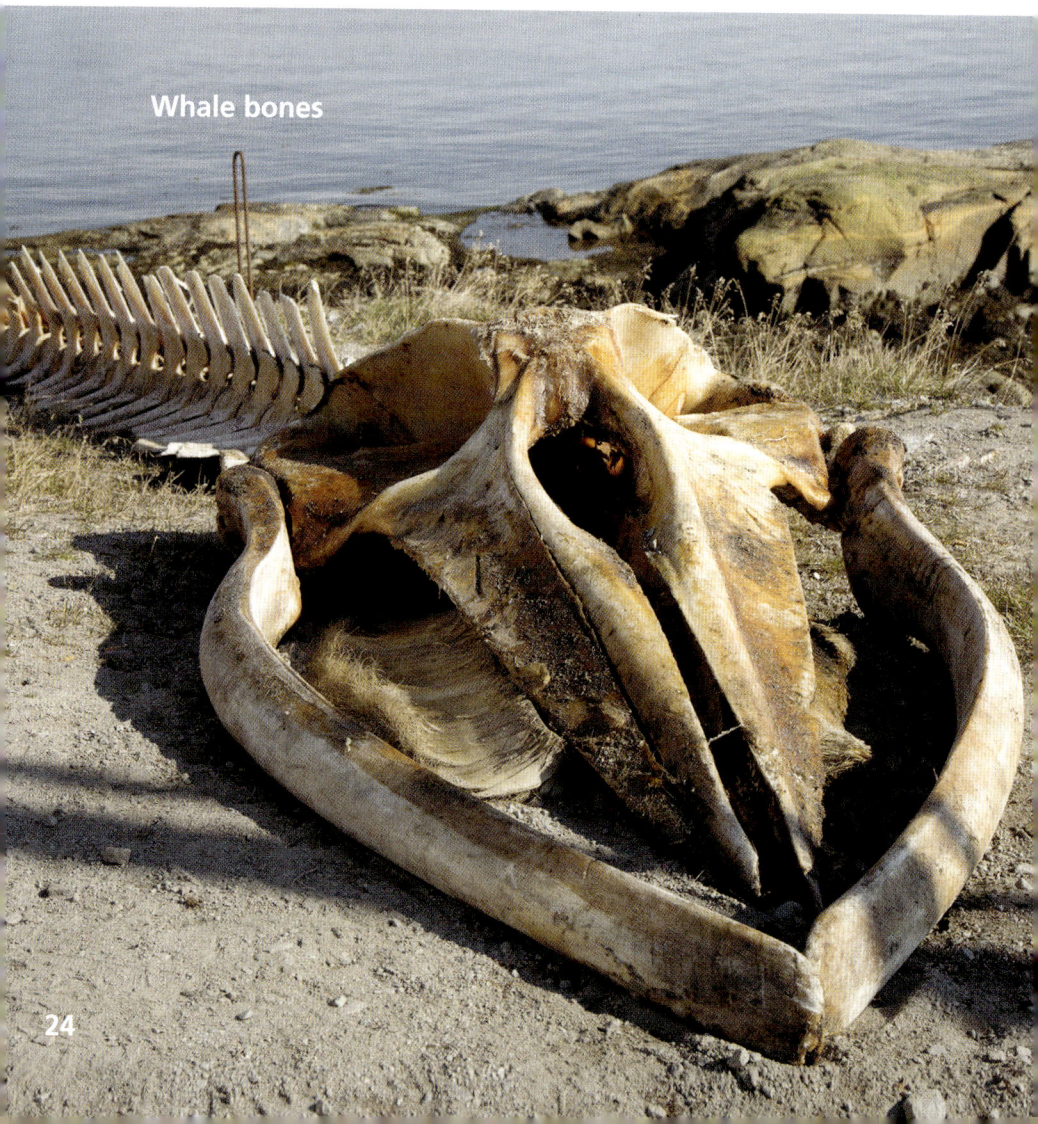

Another theory *(THEER-ree)* is that, long ago, people in some Asian countries would sometimes find whale bones washed up on shore. They may have imagined *(ih-MAJ-ind)* these bones were from a huge animal that lived in the ocean *(OH-shun)*. Many Asian dragons are associated *(uh-SOH-shee-ay-ted)* with water.

Whale bones

The Komodo *(kuh-MOH-doh)* dragon is the world's largest lizard, and some consider it to be a modern dragon.

There are several animals that have been named after dragons. These include sea dragons, bearded dragons, and dragonflies *(DRAG-gun-flyz)*. You can see why they may have been given these names.

Komodo dragons live on five small islands in Indonesia *(in-doh-NEE-zhuh)*.

SEA DRAGONS

DRAGONFLIES

BEARDED DRAGONS

Dragons can be many different sizes. Some are huge—250 feet long with a wingspan of 400 feet. That's wider than the length of a football field! Others may be as small as 18 inches in length. In one legend from China, a dragon shrinks and gets small enough *(ee-NUF)* to fit into a rice bowl!

Most dragons are shown as very big and very strong. A few have been described as gentle, but most are terrifyingly *(TARE-ih-fy-ing-lee)* fierce with big, sharp teeth.

In most dragon myths, baby dragons hatch from eggs. They grow very slowly and live a very long time. European dragons are believed to live up to 4,400 years. When they reach this age, they become ill and die. The Chinese *(chy-NEEZ)* horned dragon must wait 500 years before it is even old enough to grow its horns.

COMPARING SIZES
How big are dragon eggs?

chicken egg – 2.5 inches (6 cm)

ostrich egg – 6 inches (15 cm)

dragon egg – 12 inches (30 cm)

Dragons are thought to live in places that are hard to reach. European *(YUR-oh-PEE-un)* dragons typically *(TIP-pik-uh-lee)* live in castles *(KAS-ulz)* on top of mountains or deep inside large caves. Dragons from Asia can live in the ocean or water. Some have castles underwater. Others live in rain clouds.

Traditionally *(truh-DISH-uh-nuh-lee)*, dragons are said to live alone, but they will sometimes work together to fight a common enemy. A group of dragons is called a thunder, or a band.

CHAPTER 6

DRAGON SKILLS

Throughout (throo-OWT) history, people have described dragons' incredible (in-KRED-ih-bul) skills. These skills can be menacing (MEN-uh-sing) and scary. Some dragons can breathe fire. Some can breathe ice or venom. Some can change their shape or even change the weather. Others cause or prevent floods (fludz), rain, and storms.

While they most often appear terrifying (TARE-ih-fy-ing), some are seen as being kind. One story tells of a man who fell into a deep mountain crevice (KREV-is)—a large crack in the rock. Two dragons were spending the winter there. They fed the man and kept him warm. In the spring, they helped him to return home.

   Most European dragons have wings and can fly. Asian dragons do not usually have wings, but most of them can still fly. These wingless dragons seem to swim though the air. Legend says they stay aloft using the magic from a bump on their heads.

CHAPTER 7

DRAGON LEGENDS

A thousand years ago, the Norse people in the north of Europe *(YUR-rup)* created their own dragon myths. One legend tells of a dragon called Jormungandr *(YOR-mun-gun-dr)*, which is also known as the Midgard Serpent. This dragon terrorized the Norse people until he was cast into the ocean by their god Odin *(OH-din)*. There, the dragon grew larger and longer. He coiled around the entire world and bit his own tail. According to legend, if Jormungandr *(YOR-mun-gun-dr)* ever let go of his tail, the world would end.

Another famous *(FAY-mus)* legend comes from Central Europe. A very old and epic poem from this area features a very powerful dragon. The hero of the legend is called Beowulf *(BAY-oh-wulf)*. He battles many monsters and defeats all of them except the dragon. During his battle with the dragon, Beowulf *(BAY-oh-wulf)* is bitten. With the help of a friend, Beowulf finally defeats the dragon, but he then dies from his wounds *(woondz)*.

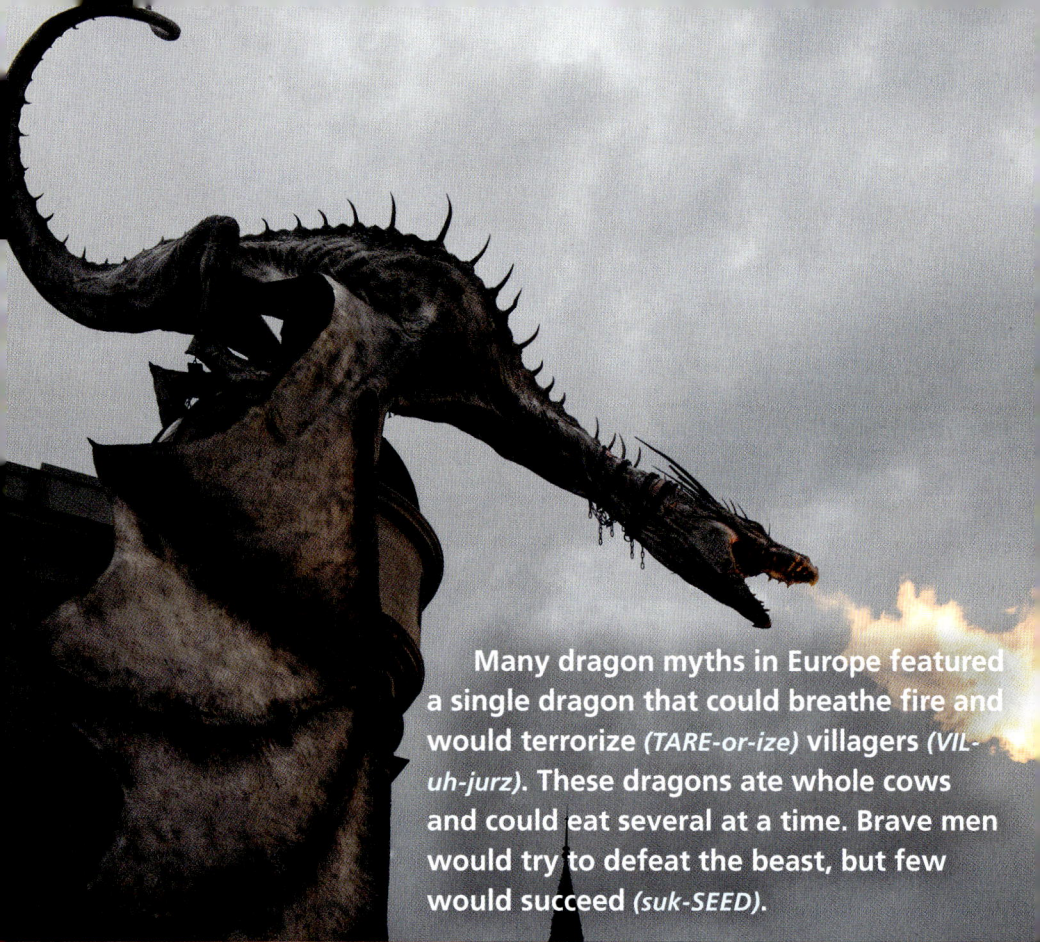

Many dragon myths in Europe featured a single dragon that could breathe fire and would terrorize *(TARE-or-ize)* villagers *(VIL-uh-jurz)*. These dragons ate whole cows and could eat several at a time. Brave men would try to defeat the beast, but few would succeed *(suk-SEED)*.

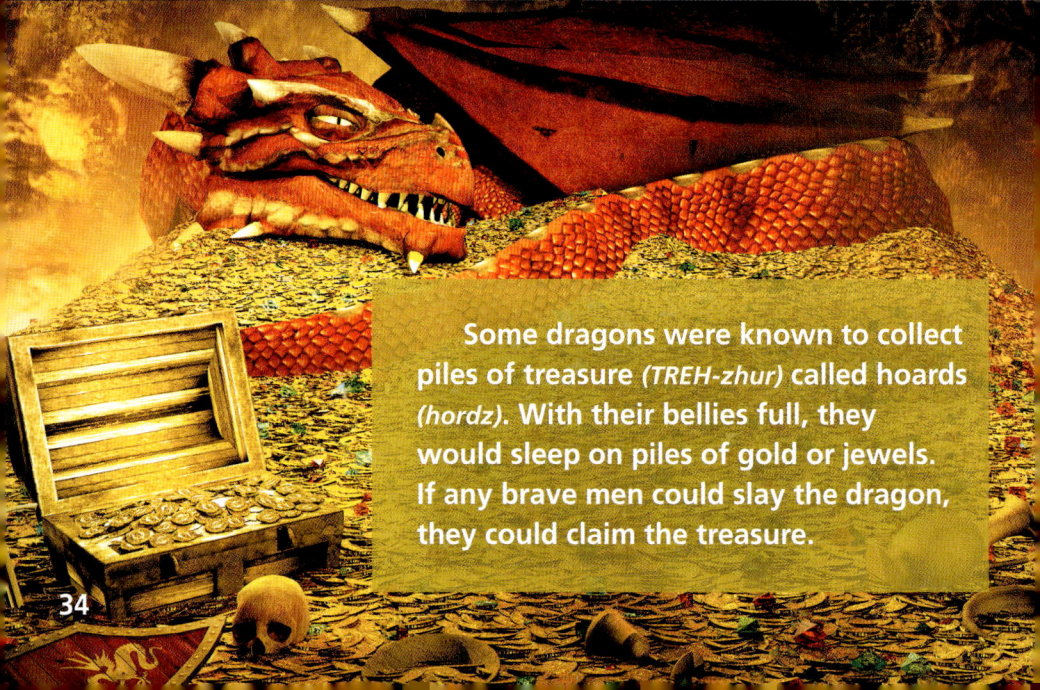

Some dragons were known to collect piles of treasure *(TREH-zhur)* called hoards *(hordz)*. With their bellies full, they would sleep on piles of gold or jewels. If any brave men could slay the dragon, they could claim the treasure.

Aboriginal *(ab-oh-RIJ-ih-nul)* people of South Australia *(ah-STRAYL-yuh)* have their own dragon myth. Akurra *(ak-YOO-rah)* is a giant water snake dragon. He has scales, sharp teeth, and a beard. It is said that the land of Australia was formed from Akurra's *(ak-YOO-rahz)* movements. He was also associated with rainfall and water. Legend tells that during a drought *(drowt)* people sneaked into Akurra's lair and took fat from his body. Then they melted the fat. The smell rose up to the sky and rain fell.

Korean *(kor-REE-un)* legends say dragons ate special orbs to give them magic powers.

Pliny *(PLIN-ee)* the Elder was a Roman scholar who believed dragons and elephants were enemies *(EN-eh-meez)*. He believed that a dragon could strangle an elephant with its tail and swallow *(SWAH-loh)* it whole. Many snakes can strangle and swallow animals bigger than themselves, but no snake is big enough to swallow an elephant!

In Japan, stories of dragons were first written down about 1,300 years ago. Most Japanese *(jap-puh-NEEZ)* dragons are gods of water. They are wise and powerful and protect *(proh-TEKT)* the oceans. These creatures can change their form, from a dragon to a human. Watatsumi *(wah-tat-SOO-mee)* is a Japanese dragon and sea god. Legends say that people who fell into the sea were welcomed into his kingdom.

The Pilatus *(pih-LAT-tis)* mountains in Switzerland *(SWIT-sur-lund)* have terrible storms. People thought dragons lived in the mountains. It was believed that dragons caused *(kawzd)* the storms.

Dragons are a sign of royalty *(ROY-uhl-tee)* in China. The emperor of China was traditionally *(truh-DISH-uh-nuh-lee)* known as "the dragon." Chinese dragons also symbolize *(SIM-boh-lize)* spring. Communities *(kum-MYOO-nih-teez)* around the world hold dragon dance parades for Chinese New Year in February *(FEB-yoo-air-ee)*.

Ancalagon *(an-KAL-a-gon)* the Black is a huge dragon from J.R.R. Tolkien's *(TOHL-keenz)* series, *The Lord of the Rings.* He led an army of dragons in a fight against a group of elves. Ancalagon *(an-KAL-a-gon)* was defeated in the battle. As he fell, his body crushed three mountains. This means Ancalagon was HUGE! But Tolkien *(TOLE-keen)* does not reveal the dragon's exact size in his writings.

Dragons are often portrayed *(por-TRAYD)* as evil *(EEV-uhl)*. In some modern stories, they are portrayed as good. But whether good or evil, dragons are almost always thought to be smart. Some people think that dragon sightings are rare because dragons are too smart to be caught. People still report dragon sightings, but they are quickly disproven *(dis-PROO-ven)*. Most dragon hunting today happens only in stories and human imagination *(ih-maj-jih-NAY-shun)*.

Could you train a dragon? In legends, some dragons are friendly, but they can also be dangerous *(DANE-jer-us)*. Dragons with so much power aren't easy to train. But intelligent *(in-TEL-ih-jent)* dragons like words games. So, if you ever meet a dragon, talk to him. Ask him to answer *(AN-sur)* a riddle or tell him a joke. It might be your best chance to get the dragon to do what you want. And always remember to be polite!

GLOSSARY

aboriginal *(ab-oh-RIJ-ih-nul)*: related to the indigenous, or native, peoples of Australia

alicorn *(AL-ih-korn)*: the horn of a unicorn

coat of arms: the official symbol of a family, state, nation, or other group

exotic *(ex-ZOT-ik)*: strange or unfamiliar

legends *(LEH-jinz)*: stories from the past that may or may not be true but cannot be checked

origin *(OR-ih-jin)*: the point where something begins

reptiles: animals that are covered in scales, usually lay legs, and are cold-blooded

scholar: a person who has spent a long time studying a particular subject

venom *(VEH-num)*: a poison that an animal uses to kill or injure another animal by biting or stinging

QUESTIONS TO THINK ABOUT

1. What are some of the real animals that may have inspired the unicorn legend? Can you think of any animals not mentioned in the book that have something about them that is similar to a unicorn? What is similar?

2. What are some of the real animals that may have inspired dragon legends? Can you think of any animals not mentioned in the book that have something about them that is similar to a dragon? What is similar?

3. Do you think dragons or unicorns may have existed? Why or why not?

4. What kind of evidence might prove that these animals existed or prove that they never existed?

5. If these animals were real, which one would you most like to see and why?

CODE READER™

Making Difficult Words Easy

Code Reader Books provide codes with "sound keys" to help read difficult words. For example, a word that may be challenging to read is "chameleon," so it might be followed by a code like this: chameleon *(kuh-MEE-lee-un)*.

The codes use phonetic keys for each sound in the word. Knowing the keys can help make reading the codes easier.

Code Reader™ Keys

Long a sound (as in make):
a *(with a silent e)*, **ai**, or **ay**
Examples: break *(brake)*;
area *(AIR-ee-uh)*; able *(AY-bul)*

Short a sound (as in cat): **a**
Example: practice *(PRAK-tis)*

Long e sound (as in keep): **ee**
Example: complete *(kum-PLEET)*

Short e sound (as in set): **e** or **eh**
Examples: metric *(MEH-trik)*;
bread *(bred)*

Long i sound (as in by):
i *(with a silent e)* or **y**
Examples: might *(mite)*;
bicycle *(BY-sih-kul)*

Short i sound (as in sit): **i** or **ih**
Examples: myth *(mith)*;
condition *(kun-DIH-shun)*

Long u sound (as in cube): **yoo**
Example: unicorn *(YOO-nih-korn)*

Short u or schwa sound (as in cup):
u or **uh**
Examples: pension *(PEN-shun)*;
about *(uh-BOWT)*

Long o sound (as in hope):
o *(with a silent e)*, **oh**,
or **o** at the end of a syllable
Examples: molten *(MOLE-ten)*;
ocean *(OH-shen)*; nobody *(NO-bah-dee)*

Short o sound (as in top): **o** or **ah**
Examples: posture *(POS-chur)*;
bother *(BAH-ther)*

Long oo sound (as in cool): **oo**
Example: school *(skool)*

Short oo sound (as in look): **o͝o**
Examples: wood *(wŏŏd)*;
could *(kŏŏd)*

oy sound (as in boy): **oy**
Example: boisterous *(BOY-stur-us)*

ow sound (as in cow): **ow**
Example: discount *(DIS-kownt)*

aw sound (as in paw): **aw**
Example: faucet *(FAW-sit)*

qu sound (as in quit): **kw**
Example: question *(KWES-chun)*

zh sound (as in garage): **zh**
Example: fission *(FIH-zhun)*